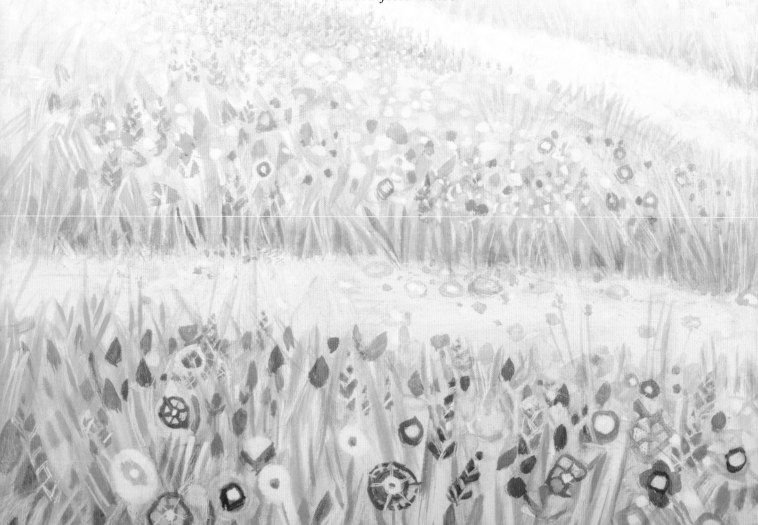

For Elsie Gail Watson, in loving memory

Thank you to models Sundee Frazier, Jesse Watson,
Dare, Daniel, Taj, Crosby, Rayna, and Gracie.

Special thanks to World Vision, Inc. for generous permission
to use photos from their library as inspiration and reference.

PSALM 23 has always been a comfort to me.
While I was painting the illustrations for this book it
made me smile to think that we are all his little lambs.
And while we often lose our way, The Good Shepherd "... calls
his own sheep by name and leads them out"— (John 10:3).
To pasture. To tranquil waters.

—Richard Jesse Watson

PSALM 23

ZONDERVAN.com/
AUTHORTRACKER
follow your favorite authors

The LORD is my shepherd; I shall not want.

He maketh me to lie down in green pastures:

he leadeth me beside the still waters.

He restoreth my soul:

he leadeth me in the paths of righteousness

for his name's sake.

Yea, though I walk through the valley
of the shadow of death,
I will fear no evil:

for thou art with me;
thy rod and thy staff they comfort me.

Thou preparest a table before me
in the presence of mine enemies:

thou anointest my head with oil;

my cup runneth over.

Surely goodness and mercy shall follow me

all the days of my life:

and I will dwell in the house of the LORD for ever.

PSALM 23

The LORD is my shepherd; I shall not want.
He maketh me to lie down in green pastures:
he leadeth me beside the still waters.
He restoreth my soul: he leadeth me in the
paths of righteousness for his name's sake.
Yea, though I walk through the valley
of the shadow of death,
I will fear no evil: for thou art with me;
thy rod and thy staff they comfort me.
Thou preparest a table before me
in the presence of mine enemies:
thou anointest my head with oil;
my cup runneth over.
Surely goodness and mercy shall
follow me all the days of my life:
and I will dwell in the house
of the LORD for ever.

ZONDERKIDZ

Psalm 23
Illustrations © 2013 by Richard Jesse Watson

Requests for information should be addressed to:
Zondervan, 5300 *Patterson Ave SE, Grand Rapids, Michigan* 49530

Library of Congress Cataloging-in-Publication Data

Psalm 23
p.   cm.
ISBN 978-0-310-72784-2
1. Bible. O.T. Psalms XXIII—Criticism, interpretation, etc.—Juvenile literature.
I. Title; Psalm twenty-three.
BS145023rd .P73 2015
223'.206—dc23   2012030652

Editor: Barbara Herndon
Cover & interior design: Kris Nelson

Printed in China

13 14 15 /DSC/ 10 9 8 7 6 5 4 3 2 1